# SOMETIMES IT'S O.K. TO TELL SECRETS!

"SOMETIMES IT'S O.K. TO TELL SECRETS! does a superb job of opening the lines of communication between parents and children. It's both entertaining and informative, and an important book."
—National Kid Watch Program
(1-800-KID WATCH)

"This book is not meant to scare but rather to educate. Children need to learn that they can tell their parents anything, especially if something is wrong. Adults, in turn, must learn to listen and must give their children the freedom to tell."
—Children's Justice Foundation, Inc.

"SOMETIMES IT'S O.K. TO TELL SECRETS! is a wonderful resource for parents and teachers to utilize in instructing children about protecting themselves from those who might victimize them. The book is clever and appealing and reinforces learning through discussions, stories, and pictures."
—Sister Georgianna Cahill, SSS, LCSW,
Administrative Director, Catholic
Youth & Community Service

# IT'S O.K. TO SAY NO!

"IT'S O.K. TO SAY NO! is a practical form of child sexual abuse prevention. It is a must for parents as well as teachers. Direct and to the point, it offers solid 'how to' suggestions in real life situations."

> —Barbara Griffith, Ph.D.
> Clinical Psychologist
> Editor for Region Nine Children, Youth
> and Families Resource Center,
> Los Angeles, CA

"As a facilitator for thoughtful parents, IT'S O.K. TO SAY NO! treads the middle ground between cynicism in dealing with a painful topic. While it intends to make children wary, it does not intend for parents to shift the full burden of responsibility for the personal, physical safety of children to the children themselves."

> —*School Library Journal*

"IT'S O.K. TO SAY NO! does an excellent job of addressing a difficult subject. A practical, real-world, non-paranoid approach makes this an invaluable aid to parents and children."

> —National Kid Watch Program
> (1-800-KID WATCH)

"An extremely valuable prevention tool for children and parents alike. We can only provide positive words for the content of this publication."

> —Robin E. Swank
> Volunteers Against Abuse Center

# SOMETIMES IT'S O.K. TO TELL SECRETS!

## A PARENT/CHILD MANUAL FOR THE PROTECTION OF CHILDREN ·

**ROBIN LENETT and DANA BARTHELME**

**with BOB CRANE**

**Illustrated by FRANK C. SMITH**

AN RGA PRODUCTION

**TOR**

A TOM DOHERTY ASSOCIATES BOOK

The stories in chapter six are works of fiction. All the characters and events portrayed in this chapter and in other examples in this book are fictional. Any resemblance to real people or incidents is purely coincidental.

SOMETIMES IT'S O.K. TO TELL SECRETS!

First printing: August 1986

A TOR Book

Published by Tom Doherty Associates
49 West 24 Street
New York, N.Y. 10010

ISBN: 0-812-59454-1
CAN. ED.: 0-812-59455-X

Library of Congress Catalog Card Number: 85-52419

Printed in the United States

0  9  8  7  6  5  4  3  2  1

# Chapter One

## Introduction

Child sexual abuse claims an unknown number of victims. An estimated 250,000 children will be reported sexually abused this year alone, but no one knows the true extent of this tragedy.

Perhaps a million and a half children will be undisclosed victims—possibly many more.

It is noteworthy that in communities where a concerted effort has been made to educate the public about the dangers of child sexual abuse, and the need for reporting molestations and attempted molestations, the number of incidents reported to authorities has risen sharply.

One of the most widely admired programs for the prevention and treatment of child sexual abuse is conducted by the city of Tacoma, Washington, and its larger governmental jurisdiction of Pierce County.

Tacoma's program was started in 1976, a year in which twenty-five cases of child sexual abuse were reported to Tacoma-area authorities. By 1984, with the program solidly entrenched in the community, the number of reported cases had risen to approximately 3,000.

The Tacoma area did not experience a one-hundredfold increase in child sexual abuse. Experts in the field believe that there has probably been little, if any, increase in the frequency of child sexual abuse. What the Tacoma area experienced was a one-hundredfold increase in the *reporting* of such incidents.

For several reasons, Tacoma's statistics are highly encouraging to the authorities who deal with this crime and its consequences.

First, those statistics demonstrate that when a community makes a well-coordinated effort to educate children and adults about the threat of child sexual abuse and its impact on the victims, the barrier of silence falls. When parents and children are made aware of what child

sexual abuse is, and how vitally important it is to help the victims of this crime, embarrassment and shame are lifted from the victims and their parents. Disclosure then becomes more acceptable than silence.

Second, disclosure means that society has an opportunity to assist the victims—to help heal the psychological wounds that might otherwise burden the victim for a lifetime. And society gets the opportunity as well to identify and deal with those who would sexually molest children—to stop them from victimizing child after child.

The experts say that we cannot eradicate the roots of child sexual abuse. Many of those who sexually molest children do so because it is their primary means of sexual expression.

This perverted sexual preference can be formed early in life. Experts say that as many as four out of five child molesters were themselves molested as children. Detective Dick Vance of the Montebello (Cal.) Police Department, who works with child sexual abuse cases on a daily basis, calls this victim-to-victimizer phenomenon "The Vampire Syndrome."

Molested children often become molesting adults, and no one fully understands why.

Consciously or unconsciously, many child molesters shape their lives on a course that accommodates this sexual drive. Some choose career paths that will bring them daily contact with children. Others regularly volunteer for activities that give them supervisory responsibilities for groups of children.

If we cannot rid our society of those who would sexually molest children, we must take whatever steps are necessary to protect our children from these criminals.

Step One is to educate ourselves, our children, and the professionals who work with our children about the dangers and the consequences of sexual abuse. Step Two is to break the barrier of silence that surrounds this crime.

Step One is vitally important because experience has shown that children who are educated about child sexual assault are better prepared to protect themselves than those who are unaware of the dangers. The informed child is also far more likely to disclose an incident than a child who only vaguely recognizes what has occurred.

Step Two is critically important because silence perpetuates the crime and leaves the victim with a potentially lifelong debilitating

psychological burden. Unless parents and child counselors are willing to listen to a child, the cycle of victimization will not be broken.

We have an obligation as parents to create an environment in which children feel free to communicate, to discuss any situation that makes them feel uncomfortable, and to disclose the occurrence of a sexual molestation.

The purpose of this book is to help parents, and others with guardianship responsibilities for children, create an environment in which children have the freedom to tell.

# Chapter Two

## Behind the Cloak of Decorum

There is nothing "typical" about the child molesters in our society. The molester may be male or female, of any age, any occupation, and as likely as not have children of his or her own.

It is easy to believe that most child molesters are strangers to the children they victimize, but the facts contradict this. About seventy-five percent of all reported sexual abuse cases involve molesters who are known and trusted by their child victims, or by the parents of the victims.

The following true story is not unusual. The man was a second grade schoolteacher, president of his local Little League, and taught Sunday school. He was a model citizen, admired by parents and loved by children.

Then a child accused him of sexual assault. The community was appalled by the accusation, and refused to believe that he could possibly have done such a thing. One by one, other children came forward and disclosed that they, too, had been victims of his sexual assaults. In all, seventeen children accused the man. He was convicted, and is serving a prison sentence.

Disclosure is the child molester's greatest fear. For that reason, the molester may consciously wrap him- or herself in the cloak of decorum. Professional counselors of abused children say that in general the molester is a despised figure, until it is discovered that a relative, a trusted friend, or an admired acquaintance has been guilty of the crime.

Under such circumstances, a person's contempt for the molester may turn to pity. The molester is driven by a perverted sexual preference, and in this regard is to be pitied, like an alcoholic or a drug addict. However, unlike alcoholics or drug addicts, who are their own victims, the molester consistently victimizes the innocents of society.

It is important to remember that a child molester rarely exhibits any remorse. The molester is convinced that his or her actions are acceptable, or beneficial to, or even desired by, his or her victims.

That is an important point. A child molester cannot be embarrassed into stopping by a parent who confronts him or her with a reasoned argument about the perversity of the actions.

If you are to help prepare for the possibility of an attempted molestation, you must understand the molester's mode of operation. How are children beguiled into doing what the molester wants? What does the molester say that prompts so many victimized children to keep silent?

There are child molesters who seize their victims by force. However, enticement, trickery, and bribery are the most common mode of operation among molesters. The molester wants first to gain the confidence of both parent and child so that the child will believe that their relationship is okay and should be kept secret.

Molesters, like other habitual criminals, have what police call a "modus operandi," a method of operation that varies little from one crime to another.

If the molester holds a position of responsibility over children, he or she may freely devote an unusual amount of time, attention, and love to the children in an attempt to create a bond.

In therapy sessions with psychologists, many convicted molesters stress that their first objective, once they have targeted a child, is to gain the confidence and trust of the parents. The molester thus establishes credibility with the parents, which in turn encourages the child to trust the molester.

Once credibility is established with parents, the molester may devote much time and effort to organizing camping trips or day outings for groups of children for the sole purpose of targeting on one child victim.

"Safety in numbers" does not guarantee that a child is protected from molestation. Molesters are well aware that a single child can easily be separated from the group, or can be dropped off late at home with a seemingly legitimate excuse.

We are not suggesting that parents be wary of group outings or activities supervised by one adult. Being paranoid about such things would have its own undesirable consequences. You cannot lock your child away from circumstances that might contain some element of risk.

That is why it is so important to educate your children about the potential of sexual assault. They can be educated to recognize a

possible assault, and they can be taught to tell you when such an incident occurs.

Whatever his or her method of operation, the molester works with several advantages. First, he or she knows that children tend to trust adults and lack the experience to attach sinister motives to a seemingly innocent enticement. Second, the molester knows that he or she can play upon children's fears of consequences—real or imagined—to coerce them into silence.

In recent years, there have been two cases of large-scale sexual abuse of children—one in New York, the other in the Los Angeles area. In the aftershock of both revelations, the same question was asked repeatedly: Why did the victims remain silent for so long?

The evidence that has come to light in both cases shows that the child victims were, in effect, terrorized into silence by threats of harm to them or to their parents.

The children believed the threats. That made them very real, and very effective. Although these were extreme cases, it is important to realize that even subtle threats (for example, the loss of parental love if a relationship is disclosed) can be terrifying in the mind of a child.

# Chapter Three

## Breaking the Silence

It is vitally important that we make children aware that there are adults who would sexually victimize them. But that isn't enough.

It is equally important that we encourage them to speak out, that we break the shell of silence that protects a child molester from public disclosure and ensures perpetuation of his crimes.

How do we give children the freedom to tell?

Let's look at the situation from the child's point of view.

A child's relationship with adults is normally infused with a deep sense of trust. After all, a child is dependent upon adults for support and guidance throughout his or her formative years. It takes time and experience to develop a defensive attitude about adult intentions.

When a child is drawn into a trusting relationship with a molester, the child has a difficult time accepting the reality of the situation. If the child has trouble believing that an adult would violate that bond of trust, how can he or she expect anyone else to believe it?

The child molester understands the child's fear and plays upon it. He may tell the child that he or she will not be believed, and that speaking to other adults will have damaging consequences for the child.

If the molester is a relative or a friend of the family, he may encourage silence by suggesting that the child will be held responsible for the consequences of disclosure—will be subject to the hatred of family and friends if the molester is prosecuted.

If the molester is a teacher or coach, the threats may be more appropriate to the circumstances (for example, poor grades or being cut from the team). Threats are terrifying to a child because his or her security in the social environment is fragile. A child molester knows

that, and can build a convincing case for silence on even the flimsiest of threats.

Above all, a child wants to maintain his or her place within the family or the social environment. If merely speaking about a sexual abuse is a danger to that security, a child will be reluctant to break the silence even though he or she may be deeply distressed.

For that reason, it is very important that your child has no doubt about his or her credibility with you and knows that he or she will be held blameless for the actions of an adult and will get your support and comfort. This kind of security can be ingrained in a child only through continual reinforcement.

The keys to breaking the silence are in security and credibility. If a child is aware that his or her security cannot be jeopardized by disclosing an attempted sexual abuse, a molester's invulnerability is considerably diminished. If a child thinks that a responsible adult will

15

believe his or her story about an attempted molestation, the child is likely to speak out.

The Tacoma experience related earlier is probably indicative of what happens when a community makes a concerted effort to deal with child sexual abuse. When children are made aware of potential situations for abuse, when their disclosures of such situations are given credibility, the number of reported abuse cases rises dramatically.

The Tacoma area has incorporated its program into the school

curriculum. The lessons of "bad touch–good touch" are begun in the early grades, and the children also learn the importance of telling a responsible adult about any improper approach.

Given the attention that has recently been focused on child sexual abuse, such lessons may one day be a standard part of school curricula everywhere.

Until then, the question is: How can you arm your child, or the children you are responsible for, with the sense of security and credibility that will encourage frankness about attempted molestations?

The answer is that you must work to create an environment of security and credibility.

17

# Chapter Four

## Security and Credibility

The adult who consistently feels secure about the love and esteem of family and friends is rare indeed. The majority is plagued with doubt.

Children are no different. However, unlike adults, who usually have a measure of independence, children are unable to sustain themselves outside the circle of family and friends. They are wholly dependent upon the adults who support them, and they are very much aware of their vulnerability.

Psychologists say that children's most common nightmare concerns the loss of parents or guardians. If the nighttime dread is the physical loss of parents or adults, the equivalent daytime fear is the loss of the love of parents or guardians.

That is where children are most insecure, and most vulnerable. That is the vulnerability that many child molesters take advantage of when they coerce silence from their victims. ("If you tell your parents about this, they won't believe you, and won't love you anymore.")

Obviously, the child who feels secure in the love of his or her parents or guardian is unlikely to accept that argument. But how many children are that secure?

Children must be constantly reassured of parental love. In the context of protecting them from sexual abuse, they must be constantly reassured that no matter what happens, parental love will not be jeopardized.

That is not to suggest that children should not be disciplined for misbehavior when it is appropriate. However, the parent who equates discipline with the withholding of love from a child is following a risky course, for that is precisely what the molester wants the child to believe when he or she encourages silence.

Many sexually abused children blame themselves for the events they are caught up in, and keep silent because they believe the responsibility is theirs. It is therefore critically important that children be made to understand that they are never to blame for the actions of an adult.

If a child believes that his or her parents fully accept responsibility for the child's protection, he or she is likely to speak up when safety and security seem at risk.

Your child develops a sense of his or her credibility in conversations with you and through experience. If you listen to your child, if you are willing to accept what he or she says at face value, the child will be open and expressive.

We know that children tend to exaggerate day-to-day events in relating them to adults. The dog they encountered on the way home

from school was bigger than life. The catch that a baseball teammate made at the Little League game defied the laws of gravity. You take these comments with a grain of salt, but it's hardly necessary to dispute them.

Ironically, police authorities have discovered that very often the best witnesses to crimes or automobile accidents are the children among the bystanders. A few years ago, New York police questioned witnesses to a street mugging. Four adult witnesses gave different—and contradictory—descriptions of the mugger. One officer approached an eight-year-old boy who had witnessed the crime. He provided a coolly detailed description.

The police found the man hiding in a nearby hallway. They said the boy's description couldn't have been more accurate if he had taken a photograph of the man.

Children may exaggerate inconsequential events. They tend not to exaggerate significant events, or those that they find troubling.

In fact, in the latter case, children tend to be circumspect. If a child cannot grasp the meaning of an event that seems somehow suspicious, he or she may take a stab at understanding it by asking an innocent question of an adult. If the answer doesn't fully satisfy the child's curiosity, he or she may simply drop the subject.

That's why it is important to listen to your child's questions, to answer them as best you can, and then ask why the question was raised. That is particularly true if the child is asking a question about an adult that he or she encounters regularly.

The biggest barrier to frankness is the risk of recrimination. If you inject an element of risk into a conversation with your child, he or she will be hesitant to be open with you in the future.

One such reaction is the "Haven't I warned you . . ." response. The child raises a question about some event or circumstance that is troubling. The child remarks, "While I was going past the video arcade this afternoon—"

You cut him off by saying, "Haven't I warned you never to go near the video arcade?"

The child's reaction is predictable. First, he will become defensive. "Well, gee, I couldn't help it because I was on my way to the bookstore, and the only way to get there is to walk past the video arcade."

By this time, the child may be reluctant to go any further with his comments. He's already been stung for where he was, and he hasn't even gotten to the troublesome part yet.

Perhaps a man came out of the video arcade and made some advances to him. Based on your reaction simply to the child's location, he would be reluctant to increase your anger by proceeding with his story.

In all likelihood, he'll retreat and make up some innocuous story so that he can back out gracefully, and the next time something occurs that troubles him, he's going to think twice about even initiating a discussion.

In a case such as this, it would probably be best simply to ignore the minor infraction—the proximity to the video arcade—and hear the child out.

A child knows the risk in admitting to something that is explicitly forbidden. The fact that the child is willing to take that risk should suggest that there is something particularly troublesome about the story that is about to be related.

If a child tells you something that contains an element of self-incrimination—admitting to being in the wrong place or with the wrong people—the child probably should be exempted from "Haven't I warned you . . ." or "I told you . . ." because that is probably not what the child is truly concerned about.

Even criminals are protected in our court system from self-incrimination. No one can be forced to testify against himself. Certainly your child deserves that much consideration.

Some children, faced with the dilemma of disclosing something that disturbs them and exposes them to a degree of risk, will impersonalize a situation, making a "friend" the subject of the event.

Such circumstances require sensitive handling. The child is trying to cope with two fears—the troubling situation itself and your reaction to it. Your most helpful response is probably to accept the impersonalized story and support your child on what the friend should do.

But keep in mind that in cases of child sexual abuse, the "friend" may indeed be a friend. Some children caught in a quandary over a sexual abuse, and with no one to turn to—particularly if they are being abused by a member of the immediate family—may tell a friend about it. Such an action represents a desperate—and pathetic—cry for help.

If you are confronted with a situation such as that, ask your child to inquire if his or her friend would come to you. Contact a local child abuse agency for guidance on how to proceed.

If, however, you suspect that your child's "friend" is merely a proxy figure for his or her experience, hear the child out, and be comforting and impersonal. If the incident in question was a relatively minor one and your counsel is calming and comforting, the child may be more forthcoming with you should there ever be another incident.

Parents are usually troubled about reporting seemingly minor incidents of sexual approach that their children are involved in if the approach was made by someone they know. Should a seemingly minor incident be reported to the police, or shouldn't it?

Authorities in the field of child sexual abuse uniformly counsel that all attempted sexual molestations—even those that seem insignificant—should be reported. There are a number of sound reasons for this.

First, because of the barrier of silence that surrounds this crime, you may not be aware that the individual identified by your child may have been previously reported to the police for similar actions.

It is helpful to the authorities to have a record of all such incidents, and they *do* maintain accurate records and cross-filing systems that allow them to keep track of attempted and acknowledged molestations.

Secondly, the sexual molestation of children is rarely limited to one incident. Most child molesters attempt the crime over and over again. Your failure to report an incident may contribute to the victimization of another child.

Third, in disclosing to you an incident of attempted molestation, your child is looking to you for protection. Your failure to report an incident may suggest to the child that you do not believe him or her—or, worse, that such incidents are not significant enough for you

to bother about. Take the advice of experts in the child counseling field, and report *any* incident of attempted sexual abuse to the police.

Incidentally, we are not suggesting that you become alarmed over the relatively innocent sexual explorations of children. "Playing doctor" with other children of the same age is a phase that most children go through. Only if an older child is involved are such activities grounds for serious concern.

In giving your child a sense of credibility and security, one response that parents should carefully avoid is "If I ever hear you say that again about . . ." As a rule, children do not gossip about adults. They can be occasionally unkind about the notable characteristics of certain adults (extreme obesity or meanness toward children, for example), but they rarely gossip with the intensity of adults.

If a child raises questions about the behavior of an adult, it is inadvisable to chastise the child about his or her comments. "Don't ever let me hear you say that about him again" has a clear meaning to the child. It means "I don't believe you" or "I respect him too much to entertain such thoughts."

It is better to follow up the child's comments with questions, calmly phrased, about what makes the child say what he or she has said.

If you want your child to be open with you about potential incidents of abuse, you must yourself keep an open mind.

If your child tells you of some incident of attempted sexual abuse (whether your child or another child was the target), it is critically important that you not express disbelief of the reported incident. Such a reaction immediately puts the child on the defensive. As a consequence, the child may retract the story rather than be subjected to skeptical parental interrogation.

It is advisable to occasionally discuss the subject of child sexual abuse at home. Such discussions may have several beneficial consequences.

First, such discussions tell the child that the subject is not too embarrassing to be discussed in the home. One of the reasons for children's silence in sexual abuse cases is their belief that anything of a sexual nature is taboo for home discussion.

Second, occasional discussion of the subject may encourage the child to express his or her concerns about a puzzling relationship with an adult.

Today's heightened awareness of the dangers of child sexual abuse offers numerous opportunities to casually introduce the subject at home. The subject comes up frequently on television news shows. Many milk companies are now putting pictures of missing children on their product cartons.

A parent should use the opportunity for such discussions to give children tips about how they can help protect themselves ("Don't get into a car with a stranger").

A parent should also use the opportunity to acquaint children with the threats that molesters use ("If you don't do what I say, I'll take your puppy away"), and to carefully explain that the parent would never allow anyone to carry out such threats.

A companion book, *It's O.K. to Say No!* (New York: Tor Books, 1985), contains a series of exercises that parents and children can do together to help the children develop an awareness of potentially dangerous situations.

# Chapter Five

## Creating an Open Environment

Ideally, you would like your child to come to you with any concerns that he or she may have.

Unfortunately, today's life-styles can make open communication between parent and child very difficult. A child is in school during the day. Often, both parents work. The family gets together briefly over dinner, then separates—homework, television, and outside activities fill the leisure hours.

If parents want to foster open communication with their children, often they must specifically make the time to do so.

One mother has created an atmosphere of openness with her two children by playing a sort of game with each one individually. She calls the game "Burden Time."

About twice a month, in private moments with one child or the other, she will say "Burden Time!" and the game will begin.

The rules are simple. Each of them, mother and child, must disclose to the other something that is bothering them at the moment. The child, for example, may talk about a deteriorating relationship with a classmate. Mother and child discuss the pros and cons of the situation, and try to work out some reasonable solution between them.

After the child's "burden" has been dealt with, it's the mother's turn to disclose some matter that is of concern to her. She keeps out of the game issues that could have some bearing on the child's sense of security, such as her financial concerns or her relationship with the divorced father.

She carefully avoids trivializing the game and does not inject insignificant worries. She may talk about the fact that she's gained five pounds and thinks she may have to go on a diet, or about the fact that

her fund-raising efforts for her club don't seem to be going as well as she had hoped.

Occasionally, she focuses her concern on the child. She'll say, "Right now, my biggest worry is you. You don't seem to be your usual self the last few days. You know I love you, and if there's

anything bothering you, it would ease my burden if you'd talk about it.''

Whether or not there is something bothering the child that hasn't been aired, the tactic is helpful. It gives the child a sense of his or her importance in the mother's life. It also makes the mother's behavior or attitudes fair game for the child's ''burden time'' disclosures. Because the mother has occasionally focused on the children, they feel free to bring up their problems with her when the circumstances are appropriate.

The son may say, "Gee, Mom, what really bothers me is that lately you've been kind of cross with me. I don't know what I've done to make you act that way." And the mother can explain that she has not been feeling well, and that there's nothing wrong with how the child has been behaving.

Under no circumstances does the mother include both children in the "Burden Time" game at the same time. She believes that a three-way discourse would seriously inhibit the children's candidness.

A critically important rule of the game is that anything discussed is strictly confidential. That rule was established at the very beginning.

If one of the children's disclosures calls for some action on the mother's part to help resolve a child's concerns, the mother gets the child's explicit approval of her strategy before proceeding.

Thus far, the woman has only once been confronted with a situation that might have been related to a potential sexual abuse. Her daughter expressed some concern about the special attention she was receiving from a male teacher. The child had an inkling that he was leading up to something she didn't like.

Mother and daughter talked about the situation and together worked out a scenario for how the child should handle an approach if it came. It never did, but the child was greatly relieved by the opportunity to talk about it.

The mother believes that her game reduces the risks of her children being sexually abused. She thinks that the children have learned to be uninhibited in expressing concern about any day-to-day event that even moderately disturbs them.

From experience, the children have learned that they will get a sympathetic ear and some helpful guidance from her. By sharing her concerns with the children, she has taught them that having personal worries and disclosing them to another individual is not a sign of weakness.

Other parents are able to elicit candidness from their children through less structured approaches. Some parents find that a drive in the family car encourages candid conversation. If they sense that a child is disturbed by something, they will suggest a trip to a store or a park, and will urge the child to talk on the way about whatever is bothering him or her.

The environment of the automobile encourages openness for several reasons.

First, two people conversing in an automobile are assured of complete privacy; the child knows that the details of a conversation cannot be overheard.

Second, with parent and child seated side by side, the child does not have to cope with the potential intimidation that is an element of face-to-face conversation. Whether child or adult, when we speak with someone who is an authority figure, we tend to analyze facial expressions or body language for clues to the person's reactions. If we read a negative reaction, we may retreat from full candidness.

In a parent-child conversation in a car, the parent's attention is partially focused on the road and the child has little opportunity to judge parental reaction from facial expression. That may be an important reason why some parents have found a quiet drive to be a valuable setting for a candid conversation. Keep in mind that it may be possible to achieve similar results by taking a long walk.

If either strategy is to be successful, it is important that during the conversation your comments should be nonjudgmental. In other words, while the child is relating his or her story, your end of the conversation should be limited to comments that move the story along or probe gently for details.

Open communication requires more than a meaningful dialogue between parent and child. Remember that actions speak louder than words, and children tend to be clever interpreters of actions.

An essential lesson for children is that their bodies are their own, and that no one has the right to touch them if they don't want to be touched.

We tend to habitually insist that children engage in physical expressions of affection for relatives and friends, even if the child is reluctant to hug "Uncle Joe" or "Mrs. Thompson." By insisting on such physical expressions of affection, we subtly suggest that adults have a right to physical contact simply because they are adults.

Let your child volunteer such physical demonstrations of affection. Don't insist on them, and don't make apologies if a child is not forthcoming with an adult. If your apologies are condescending ("Oh, she's not in a hugging mood today"), it may suggest to the child that he or she is behaving improperly by withholding an expression of affection.

The professionals who counsel child abuse victims say that it is very important that parents develop a sensitivity to changes in their children's moods and attitudes. Many children who keep their concerns

closely guarded will nevertheless telegraph their worries by noticeable changes in their personalities.

Children's moods often change from day to day, and such changes should not be cause for concern, but if a particular mood change runs several days, it should be grounds for concern and inquiry.

Major mood changes may be symptomatic of concern over a traumatic event in a child's life. Sexual abuse is one such traumatic event. Experts in the field of child sexual abuse say that when a child suffers the trauma of even attempted abuse, his or her private efforts to cope with it often manifest themselves in significant changes in mood or behavior.

Such a child may become withdrawn or cross, may change from quiet to boisterous in nature, may alter his or her eating or sleeping habits, or may suddenly become prone to bouts of bedwetting or crying. Abrupt changes can be indicative of many problems. A parent should be alert to such signals, and should gently attempt to find out what is causing the child's reaction.

Parents should also remember that open communication is fostered by their genuine interest in a child's activities. The experts say that the risk of sexual abuse is reduced by a parent's personal interest in a child's school and extracurricular activities.

It is helpful for parents to become acquainted with adults who have supervisory responsibilities for a child; however, the pressures of day-to-day living often make that impossible. Alternatively, parents can create a protective environment by encouraging children to openly discuss school and extracurricular activities at home.

That requires expressing a real interest in what a child is doing while under the supervision of other adults. It is human nature for adults who have a close personal relationship to want to discuss their daily experiences. Children are no different.

A parent's lack of interest in a child's activities outside the home sends a message to the child that those experiences are too inconsequential for discussion. If the child encounters a troubling situation in those activities, he or she may conclude that it is his or her responsibility to deal with the problem.

When a parent has shown an interest in a child's experiences away from home, the child will tend to be openly communicative.

# Chapter Six

The following pages contain a series of stories you can read to your children. They are intended to heighten a child's awareness that he or she can, and should, bring any concerns to your attention.

The stories cover a mixture of subjects. Some of them relate to attempted sexual abuse; others do not. All of them are intended to make the point that open communication between parent and child can be beneficial to the child.

We suggest that you read the stories yourself first, and eliminate those that might be inappropriate to your child's age and experience. Some of the stories related to sexual abuse may seem strong for a child to have to deal with, but they are realistic and are not uncommon experiences for children. Use your own judgment as to whether each story is appropriate for your child. In addition, you may want to change the characters' names or the situations to make them seem more realistic.

We also suggest that you not attempt to read all of these stories at one sitting. Stop when your child is no longer actively interested in listening.

The children in these stories always behave in the right way—they bring events that concern them to a parent's attention. Each story ends with the question "What would you do?" Your child should answer that he or she would tell you about the situation.

These stories are a sort of game—but they are also a rehearsal for real life.

# BRANDON'S STORY

Brandon was sitting on a hillside in the park one day when he saw a man he knew walking down the street. The man lived a block away from Brandon's home.

The man looked around to see if anyone could see him. Brandon was sitting out of his sight. When the man thought there was no one around, he broke the window of a car parked on the street and quickly stole the radio, then ran away.

Brandon didn't know what to do. He knew it would be right to tell someone what he saw, but he was frightened. He thought maybe the man would hurt him if he told.

He didn't say anything when he got home. He just thought and thought. Then he remembered his father saying that if good people didn't speak up when they saw something wrong, the bad people would never be stopped.

He went to his father and told him what he had seen. Brandon also told his father that he was scared.

His father said, "Brandon, it's my job to take care of you, to make sure that nobody hurts you.

You've done the right thing, and I'm going to tell the police what you saw. You have nothing to worry about. Speaking up about anything that's wrong is something we all should do. You've done the right thing, Brandon. You have good reason to be proud."

Brandon was proud. He was glad he spoke to his father about it.

What would you do?

43

# GINA'S STORY

Gina always wanted to have a dog. Her parents weren't too keen about it because the family lived in an apartment building and didn't have a lot of room.

Gina insisted that a little dog would be no trouble. She said she would take care of it, and it wouldn't be a bother to anyone else.

Finally, on her eighth birthday, her parents gave her a cute little fuzzy, long-eared puppy. Gina loved it and took very good care of it.

One day the assistant superintendent, Mr. Mcleod, started talking to Gina in the lobby of her building. He was saying some strange things, so Gina started walking away from him.

Suddenly Mr. Mcleod said, "Don't you have a dog? You're not supposed to have one in this building."

Gina said, "But lots of other people in the building do."

Mr. Mcleod said, "That doesn't matter. If you don't do exactly what I tell you to do, I can arrange to have the dog taken away."

Mr. Mcleod wanted Gina to come to his
apartment, but instead, Gina ran up to her
apartment and told her mom what happened.

"No one is going to take your puppy away,"
her mom said. "And I'm going to talk to
the superintendent and to the police about

Mr. Mcleod. Don't you worry at all about this."

    Gina loved her puppy. It would break her heart if he were taken away. She knew her mom wouldn't let that happen. She was glad she had told her mom about what Mr. Mcleod had said.

    What would you do?

# LEWIS'S STORY

Every summer, Lewis went to camp for three weeks. Lewis loved it, because it gave him a chance to get away from the city and to see the mountains and the woods, which he enjoyed a lot.

Some of the other kids complained about the food at the camp, but Lewis didn't mind. One walk in the woods where Lewis could see birds and animals made up for any kind of bad food.

The year he was nine years old, Lewis went away to camp again. As usual, he had a new counselor, named Brad. Lewis thought Brad was O.K. One evening when Lewis went for a walk in the woods, Brad came along.

After they had walked for a while, Brad started making some strange suggestions to Lewis. Lewis said, "No, absolutely not," and he stormed back to the camp. Brad caught up to him and apologized. Then Brad began to plead with Lewis not to tell anyone what Brad had said. "I'll lose my job if you do," he said. "Please keep it a secret."

Lewis thought about it in his bunk that night. He thought about it and thought about it. Lewis decided that he had to tell the camp's head counselor about it. Lewis thought, "What if Brad does that to some other kid who isn't as smart

as I am? I have an obligation to protect the other kids."

Lewis told the head counselor the whole story the next morning.

The man said, "Lewis, you've got a good head on your shoulders. You've done the right thing, and I know it wasn't easy. I'll take care of Brad—he won't work here anymore. You may have saved some younger boy from a terrible experience. You should be very proud of the way you handled this."

Lewis didn't feel especially proud. He felt mostly sad about it. But he knew he had no choice. It was the right thing to do.

What would you do?

# NATALIE'S STORY

Natalie was eight years old, and lived just a few blocks from her school. She was happy about that because it meant she could walk to school and didn't have to take the school bus.

One day as she was walking home, a strange man started walking with her. As they walked, he talked to Natalie and asked her silly questions. When she got home, she went into the house and locked the door behind her. The man went away.

When her mom came home from work, Natalie didn't say anything.

The next day, it happened again. Now Natalie was getting a little scared. She didn't want to tell her mom about it because she knew her mom couldn't afford to take time off from work.

As she was walking home the third day, Natalie saw the man waiting up ahead. She turned around and headed back to school. Natalie thought about taking a different street home, but the only other way was across a

dangerous road, and her mom didn't want her to go that way.

Natalie sat down on the grass and wondered

what to do. Should she call her mom at
work? Natalie looked up and there was a
policeman standing in front of her. She knew

him because he sometimes directed traffic at school.

"Are you waiting for someone, young lady? You look as though you have a problem," he said.

Natalie told him about the man, and how scared she was to walk home.

The policeman said, "Well, I think we can take care of that. Come on. I'll walk with you."

When they saw the man, the policeman said to Natalie, "Wait here." He walked over and talked with the man. When he came back, he said to Natalie, "I don't think you have to worry about him anymore, but if he ever does anything that bothers you, tell me."

The policeman walked Natalie the rest of the way home. He told her, "No one has the right to do anything that makes you feel frightened. If anyone does, don't hesitate to speak up. Tell your mom, tell a policeman, tell someone in authority. That's your right, young lady."

Natalie felt better. She had her walk home to herself again, and she enjoyed it.

What would you do?

# KYLE'S STORY

Kyle loved baseball. It was practically all he ever thought about besides his schoolwork. Kyle's dad loved baseball, too, and the two of them often watched games together on television.

Kyle tried out for his grammar school baseball team, and his dad encouraged him a lot.

On the last day of tryouts, the coaches posted a list of the kids who made the team. Kyle's name wasn't on the list. He wasn't on the team. Kyle was crushed. What would he tell his dad? He'd be so disappointed that Kyle hadn't made the team.

Kyle thought about making up some excuse. He thought maybe he could say the coaches liked the other two boys who tried out for his position better than him. He thought maybe he should say the coaches weren't fair to him.

That evening when his dad came home, he said to Kyle, "What's the matter, son? You look kind of down in the mouth."

Kyle decided to be honest about it. "I didn't

make the team, Dad. I just wasn't good enough. I'm really sorry."

His dad said, "Gee, I'm really sorry to hear about that, Kyle. I know how much you wanted to make the team. I hope you're planning to try again next year—and now you and I have a whole year to work on your hitting!" He smiled.

Kyle said, "You mean you're not disappointed in me?"

His dad said, "Disappointed? Not at all. I know you gave it your best try, and I'm proud of you. Hey, do you realize there's a good game on TV tonight?"

Kyle felt much better. He decided he was going to work hard on his hitting. Maybe next year he'd make the team. He was happy that he talked it over with his dad.

What would you do?

# VICKY'S STORY

Vicky's two closest friends were Elena and Jody. They were all the same age—eleven— and they hung around together all the time. Sometimes they would go to Jody's house and listen to their favorite music.

Jody's parents both worked, so the house was empty most of the day. Now and then Jody's older brother, Philip, would hang around with them. He was fourteen and almost in high school. Vicky thought he was O.K., even though he was a little too opinionated, and sometimes made some nasty remarks about Vicky's favorite rock stars.

One day, Philip said, "Hey, would you girls like to see something really interesting?" He took a video cassette out of a closet, and turned on the VCR.

Vicky didn't know what to expect. Suddenly she realized that it was an X-rated movie. She had never seen one before, and what she saw embarrassed her. She didn't want to seem like a nerd, so she just sat there, hoping it would be over as quickly as possible.

Vicky couldn't even look at Elena and Jody. She didn't know what their reaction was. After it was over, Philip said, "There's more of these. Next time you're here, I'll show you another."

Vicky didn't know what to do. She only knew she didn't want to go through that again. By the time she got home, it was really bothering her.

At first, she didn't want to tell her parents because she was afraid they would be angry with her. Finally, she spoke to her dad about it.

Her dad said, "It was wrong of Philip to do that. I can understand your embarrassment. What you don't realize is that Elena and Jody probably felt exactly as you did, but were afraid to say anything for the same reason you were. Talk to them about it tomorrow. The three of you can tell Philip that if he tries it again, his parents will be told about it."

Vicky talked it over with Elena and Jody. She was surprised to learn that they were just as embarrassed as she was. They agreed that if Philip tried it again, they were going to speak up and put a stop to it.

What would you do?

# ROCKY'S STORY

Rocky was in the first grade. He walked to school every day. It wasn't very far from his house, only a few blocks, and Rocky liked the walk when the weather was good.

One day, he was almost all the way to school when he realized that he had forgotten to bring his homework with him. He ran back home, got his homework, and ran to school.

By the time he got back to school, all the crossing guards were gone, and Rocky was very late. How could he go into class late without an excuse from his mom?

Rocky panicked. He didn't know what to do. He didn't want anyone to see him, so he hid in the alleyway behind the supermarket.

He was there when Mr. Carlson, who worked in the store, came out to get some boxes. He said, "What are you doing here, Rocky? Why aren't you in school?"

Mr. Carlson had a strange expression on his face as he looked at Rocky. He said, "You're in big trouble, young man. You're playing hooky. I

have a good mind to report you, but I won't if you do what I tell you."

Mr. Carlson suggested some strange things to Rocky. Now Rocky was really scared. He didn't want to do what Mr. Carlson suggested, but he didn't want to be reported either. Suddenly he just grabbed his books and ran out of the alleyway and all the way home.

When he got home, he told his mom everything. She said, "Rocky, you did the right thing. I'm going to talk to someone about Mr. Carlson. But in the meantime, let's get you to school."

Rocky felt bad about hiding when he was late for school, but he felt good about telling his mom what happened.

What would you do?

# JACLYN'S STORY

Jaclyn's best friend in the world was Krissy. They hung around together. They liked the same things, the same rock stars. Neither one liked math, but they enjoyed most of their other school subjects. They were real pals.

One day Krissy acted very strangely. She ignored Jaclyn in the schoolyard. When Jaclyn started to say something to Krissy before class, Krissy said, "I don't want to talk to you anymore."

Jaclyn was crushed. She moped through school that day. When she got home, she went straight to her room and closed the door.

When her mom came into her bedroom, she said, "Jaclyn, what's wrong with you? You don't seem yourself today."

Jaclyn wasn't going to tell her Mom about Krissy. But suddenly she blurted it out, "Krissy doesn't want to talk to me anymore, and I don't know why."

Her mom said, "Oh, Jaclyn, sometimes friends go through things like this. It's probably just a

misunderstanding. The best way to deal with things like this is to go straight at them. Call Krissy on the phone. Tell her she's your best friend and you want to know what's wrong."

Jaclyn did that. It was just a misunderstanding. They were best friends again. Jaclyn was glad she told her mom. She realized that sometimes it takes another person to help you solve your problems.

What would you do?

# STEVEN'S STORY

One day, Steven got into a fight in the schoolyard. It wasn't his fault—a boy he hardly knew started picking on him. Steven took a couple of punches, and he also gave a couple, and the fight was over very quickly.

Steven had a cut lip. The other boy had a bloody nose. But Steven had ripped the knee in his pants when he slipped during the fight.

He thought his mom would be really angry with him, so he took the long way home, trying to figure out what to do. He sat and watched the cars go by on the highway for a while, thinking about what to say to his mom.

Finally, when he knew it was almost time for dinner, he slowly walked home.

When his mom saw him, she said, "Oh, Steven, what happened to you?"

Steven said, "I'm sorry, Mom, I got into a fight at school. It wasn't my fault. I didn't start it. I'm very, very sorry."

His mom said, "Oh, my heavens, let's clean you up and put some ice on that lip of yours."

While she was fixing his lip, his mom said, "Steven, I know boys get into fights sometimes. I don't want you ever to be afraid to come home and tell me. I love you and I want to help you."

Steven was glad he told his mom. And he was glad he didn't make up a story about falling down and hurting himself. He decided that telling the truth was the easiest thing to do.

What would you do?

# TERESA'S STORY

Teresa was seven years old. She loved the big park in her neighborhood. There were swings and slides, and she could watch people playing baseball or tennis or soccer. If she wanted to, she could just lie on the grass under a big tree and watch the clouds go by.

One day as she was walking through the park, she saw Mr. Burns from her neighborhood sitting on a bench talking to another man. She liked Mr. Burns. He was always very friendly.

When she walked by, she said, "Hi, Mr. Burns." He saw her and said, "Hey, there's my favorite girl. How are you, Teresa? Come over here and sit on my lap and talk to me."

Teresa didn't want to sit on anyone's lap. She said, "No thanks, Mr. Burns."

He said, "Oh, are you going to be nasty to me? Come on over here and sit on my lap and talk a bit."

Teresa said, "No, I don't want to, Mr. Burns," and she walked away. Then Teresa started

feeling bad about what she did. She started to
think that maybe Mr. Burns wouldn't like her
anymore. When she got home, she told her mom
what happened.

Her mom said, "Teresa, you did the right
thing. No one has the right to touch you in any

way if you don't want them to—and that includes sitting on someone's lap. You have the right to choose whose lap you sit on."

Teresa felt better right away. She was glad she told her mom what happened.

What would you do?

# TOMMY'S STORY

Tommy rode the local bus to school every day. Each morning at eight o'clock sharp, he stood in front of his house, waiting for the bus. His home was near the start of the bus route, so he always got a seat by the window.

One day, a man got on at the next stop. Though there were plenty of seats on the bus, he sat right next to Tommy.

After a while, he started pressing his knee against Tommy's leg, and talking to Tommy. It made Tommy very uncomfortable. He wouldn't talk to the man, but the man kept asking questions. Finally, when his stop came, Tommy ran off the bus and into school.

Two days later, the same thing happened. Soon Tommy was afraid to get on the bus.

Tommy thought that he couldn't complain to anyone, since the man wasn't really doing anything bad.

Finally, Tommy got so upset about it, he told his mom what was happening.

His mom said, "Tommy, if that happens again, you get up and move to another seat. If the man follows you, you tell the bus driver that the man is bothering you. No one has the right to make you feel uncomfortable. If it happens again, you tell me, and I'll make sure that's the end of it."

Tommy felt a lot better. He knew that his mom would see to it that he wasn't bothered. He was happy that he told her about his problem.

What would you do?

# EMMY'S STORY

Emmy was seven years old. Her mom and dad both worked, so after school Emmy would stay at a neighbor's house until her parents came home in the evening.

That went on for about a year. Then Emmy's mom and dad decided it was better to hire a sitter for those few hours. Emmy thought the sitter, Mrs. Cartwright, was okay, but nothing special. She was big and bossy, and she didn't seem to like kids a lot. Emmy just stayed away from her, and the first week went all right.

In the second week, Emmy noticed Mrs. Cartwright going through her mom's things in the dresser of her parents' bedroom. Mrs. Cartwright didn't know Emmy had seen her. Later, Emmy saw Mrs. Cartwright take a few coins out of her mom's coin cup in the kitchen.

This time, Mrs. Cartwright noticed that Emmy had seen her. She put the money back. Then she turned to Emmy and threatened to hurt her if Emmy told her parents what happened. Emmy was so frightened, she could feel herself shake.

When her parents came home, Emmy didn't
say anything about Mrs. Cartwright. She
thought about it and thought about it.
Finally, even though it made her feel a

little sick to her stomach, Emmy decided that she had to tell.

When she finished explaining what happened, Emmy told her mom and dad that she was frightened of Mrs. Cartwright.

Her mom said, "Emmy, Mrs. Cartwright had no right to do what she did. You did the right thing in telling us. You've protected us, and I'm proud of you."

Her dad said, "If anyone ever threatens you again, you come and tell us, because it's our responsibility to protect you. You have nothing to worry about from Mrs. Cartwright. You'll never see her in this house again."

For the first time since Mrs. Cartwright left, Emmy felt good. She knew she had nothing to worry about.

What would you do?

# SKIP'S STORY

Skip was seven and a half years old and he was crazy about animals. He loved dogs and cats of all kinds and sizes. He hoped that one day he could be a veterinarian and spend all his time taking care of them.

Skip's family had a cat called Nana. Nana was a big fat furry cat who didn't like people all that much. When Skip was around the house, Nana seemed to be hiding somewhere, and she always squirmed away when Skip tried to pet her.

Mr. Warner, who lived down the street from Skip, had a puppy named Champ, and he liked to play. Skip would pass by Mr. Warner's house on the way home from school. If he saw Champ in the yard, Skip would stop and play with the puppy for a while. Mr. Warner didn't mind.

One day when Skip was playing with Champ, Mr. Warner stopped to talk. He told Skip that any time he wanted, he could come into the yard and play with Champ. Then he told Skip that he liked him so much, he wanted to give him a little

present. Mr. Warner gave Skip five dollars, and said he could spend it any way he wanted.

He told Skip to keep it a secret between the

two of them—just their special secret. The next
week, the same thing happened. Skip thought he
was rich.

But Skip remembered that his mom had told him never to take money or gifts from anyone without telling her about it. At first, he thought Mr. Warner was his friend, so it was all right not to tell. But the more Skip thought about it, the more worried he became. Why, he wondered, would Mr. Warner want to give me all that money, and why does it have to be a secret?

Finally, he told his mom about it.

She said, "Skip, it's good that you told me about this. Adults don't have secrets with children. I'll speak with Mr. Warner about this. I don't want you taking money from Mr. Warner or any other adult. I'm very pleased that you told me about this."

Skip felt better. He knew that something didn't seem quite right about taking money from Mr. Warner. He realized that telling his mom about it was a good idea.

What would you do?

# PATTY'S STORY

Every year after school was over, Patty's church took the kids in the congregation on a three-day outing in the mountains. Patty went to her first outing when she was seven, and loved it. Now she was eight and it was almost summer again.

During the trip, the whole group would stay at cabins on a big lake. They would swim, and walk through the woods, and play all kinds of games.

Even though she had loved last year's outing, Patty didn't want to go again. This year, Patty was going to have a new supervisor, Mr. Riordian, and she didn't like him. Patty knew him from some church activities, and the way he looked at her and talked to her scared Patty.

She knew that her mom and dad expected her to go on the outing, but the closer it got, the more unhappy Patty became. She didn't know what to do.

Finally, a week before the outing, her mom sensed that something was bothering Patty and asked her about it. At first, Patty wouldn't say

anything, but then she just blurted out her feelings about Mr. Riordian.

Her mom said, "Patty, if you feel that way, you shouldn't go on the trip. The whole purpose of the outing is for you to have a good time. If you're going to feel uncomfortable about it, you certainly don't have to go. Your dad and I will find interesting things for you to do here. And

don't feel guilty about not liking Mr. Riordian. He may be perfectly O.K., but you have a right to your feelings about anyone."

Patty was very relieved. She was glad she told her mom about how she felt.

What would you do?

# BARRY'S STORY

Barry was twelve and in the sixth grade. His schoolwork was good, except for math. Barry had a problem with that, so his mom and dad hired a tutor to help him.

The tutor's name was Mr. Watters. Barry's mom and dad thought Mr. Watters was just great. They said wonderful things about him all the time.

After a couple of weeks of tutoring, Mr. Watters started acting kind of strange with Barry. He said things that made Barry feel creepy, and he put his arm around Barry and got a little too close, which made Barry feel even worse.

Barry was feeling more and more uncomfortable with Mr. Watters, but he didn't know what to do. His mom and dad liked Mr. Watters so much that Barry was afraid they wouldn't listen to him.

Barry felt like a nervous wreck just before each tutoring lesson, and finally he couldn't stand it anymore. He went to his dad and told him how he felt. Barry expected his dad to say

something like, "Oh, you're just imagining things. Mr. Watters is a wonderful tutor."

Barry was surprised to hear his dad say, "Why didn't you tell me about this sooner, Barry? If that's the way you feel, we'll find another tutor for you. If you are uncomfortable with Mr. Watters, you're not going to make the kind of progress we hope for on your math lessons. That's the most important thing.''

Barry felt relieved, but then he wondered why he didn't tell his parents about his feelings sooner. He decided that maybe the best thing to do when something bothers you is to speak up before it becomes a real problem.

What would you do?

# DENISE'S STORY

For her tenth birthday, Denise's mom and dad gave her a special present. It was a little gold heart with a tiny diamond in the center, hanging from a fine golden chain. Denise loved it. For weeks, she wore it all the time, and was very proud of it.

One day in school, Denise discovered to her horror that her necklace was gone. She looked everywhere for it. She even put a note on the school bulletin board, offering a reward to anyone who found it. No one did.

Denise was heartbroken. She was afraid to tell her mom and dad because she just knew they would be very angry with her for losing such a special and expensive present.

She was worried that one of them would notice that she wasn't wearing her heart, so she tried to stay away from her mom and dad as much as possible. She even started wearing a big sweater over her blouse at home so the missing heart wouldn't be noticeable.

Then one day her dad said, "Denise, you've

been acting very strange lately. Is anything wrong?"

Denise said, "No, no, everything is fine."

Her dad said, "Are you sure? If anything is

bothering you, I wish you'd let me know,
because maybe I can help."

Denise couldn't stand it anymore. Tears came
to her eyes, and she blurted out the whole story.

Her dad said, "Oh, Denise, I'm so sorry to hear that."

Denise said, "It just fell off someplace and I didn't see it happen. I'm really sorry."

Her dad said, "You couldn't help it. The chain probably broke when you were too busy to notice. Those things happen, and you shouldn't blame yourself. I'll go back to the store, and I might just be able to find another heart like it—maybe not exactly the same, but we'll see."

Suddenly Denise felt a lot better. She took off the big sweater she was wearing, and it felt as though she was lifting a big burden from her shoulders. Sometimes, she decided, the best thing to do is to come right out and talk about the problems that really bother you.

What would you do?

# JOEL'S STORY

Joel was seven, and he believed he had the biggest problem in the entire world. His older brother, Bill, was in the hospital after an automobile accident. Joel believed that it was his fault.

Just before the accident, Joel was playing in the schoolyard, forgot about the time, and missed his school bus. He called home and his mom told Bill to drive to school and pick up Joel. That's when the accident happened.

So, Joel blamed himself. He thought that Bill and his mom and dad would never forgive him for missing the school bus. At night in bed, he prayed that he could turn back time and do it all over again. This time he wouldn't miss the school bus, and Bill would be okay.

Joel's mom and dad were concerned about Bill, so at first they didn't notice that Joel was very upset.

Then one evening just before dinner, Joel's dad said to him, "Bill is going to be okay, Joel. You don't have to look so worried."

Joel said, "I know, Dad. But the accident was

my fault because I missed the school bus. I really feel bad about it."

"Your fault?" Joel's dad said. "Of course it wasn't your fault."

Joel said, "But if I hadn't missed that school bus, Bill wouldn't have been driving."

His dad thought about it for a minute and said, "Joel, that is what is known, in scientific terms, as dumb thinking. What if Bill had been driving to basketball practice when the accident happened? Would you blame his coach? Of course not. You are not to blame for the accident because you had no power to cause it or prevent it. No one would even think to blame you for it—not your mom, not Bill, not me."

Joel was relieved. He realized that sometimes you can cause a lot of unnecessary trouble for yourself by just bottling your worries inside. He was glad he talked about his problem with his dad.

What would you do?

# LORETTA'S STORY

Loretta's teacher asked her to help out in the
fund-raising drive for the school's new gymnasium.
Loretta, who was ten, was happy to be asked.
When the volunteers were asked what they
wanted to do, she offered to take on the job of
going door to door selling raffle tickets. It was a
job most of the other kids didn't want.

Loretta was very good at it. She liked
people, and many of the families she called
on were happy to take tickets to help the
school.

One day on her rounds, Loretta rang the
doorbell in a neighborhood that was unfamiliar to
her. A woman answered the door. When Loretta
told her what she was there for, the woman
asked her to come in.

Loretta was offered a soda. At first, she
politely refused. But the woman insisted, so
Loretta said yes. As the woman handed Loretta
the soda, she bumped against a table and a
vase fell off the table and smashed on the floor.
Loretta was stunned. The woman blamed her for

the accident, even though Loretta was sure it
wasn't she who caused it.

Finally, the woman calmed down, and told
Loretta she could make up for the damage by
doing what she was told. Then the woman made
some strange suggestions that Loretta didn't like
at all. When Loretta said no, the woman said
that Loretta's parents would have to pay for the
vase. Loretta ran out of the house and hurried
home.

Loretta decided she couldn't tell her mom about it. It was probably an expensive vase. But it bothered her so much that she changed her mind and told her mom after all.

Her mom said, "Loretta, you didn't do anything wrong. That woman did. Don't ever make the mistake of doing something you know is wrong just because you think you owe something to someone. You did the right thing in telling me about it. Now, I'd like to have the address of that house, because I'm going to speak to someone about this incident."

What would you do?

# MARK'S STORY

Mark was in the sixth grade. He liked school, but he especially liked playing on his school's soccer team. He was learning the game very quickly. He thought that he would be good enough in a year or two to be a starting player on the team.

Mr. Patterson, the team's coach, made the players work very hard, but he was fair and everyone liked him.

One day, Mr. Patterson told Mark that he had something very special for Mark. He told Mark to come to his home the next day, after practice.

Mr. Patterson said that Mark should keep it a secret from everyone else. He said that if the other boys knew he was giving Mark special attention, they would be very upset.

On his way home that evening, Mark thought about what the coach had said. His dad had told him that there was no reason for adults to ask children to keep secrets unless it was a surprise party, or something like that.

Mark was worried what Mr. Patterson would think if he told the secret. But then he thought, "Well, I'll tell my dad anyway."

When his dad heard about it, he said, "I'm glad you told me, Mark. You're right, adults don't have secrets with children. Don't you worry about it. You don't have to go to Mr. Patterson's home tomorrow. I'll take care of this."

Mark felt very relieved. He was happy he told his dad about what Mr. Patterson said.

What would you do?

# ROBYN'S STORY

Robyn was at her friend Jeanne's house. She and Jeanne were both ten, and were good friends. They were working together on a school science project.

Jeanne's mom had gone out for the afternoon. The only other person in the house was Jeanne's brother, Michael, who was in high school.

While the two girls were working, Michael poked his head into the room and took a picture of them. They were startled by the flash, because they hadn't seen him.

Michael pointed the instant camera at them again, and Jeanne struck a crazy pose. They all laughed when they saw the picture. Michael asked them to do more crazy poses, and they did.

Then Michael got a little weird. He suggested that the girls take their clothes off and pose for him. Jeanne started to do it. When she saw Jeanne's reaction, Robyn started to do the same thing.

Michael took a picture, and Robyn suddenly realized that she shouldn't have her clothes off. She put her clothes back on, and told Jeanne to get dressed too. Michael said, "I already have one picture of you two. If you don't pose for more, I'll show everyone this picture."

Robyn got her things and went home. She immediately told her mom what happened. Her mom said, "You were right to put a stop to that right away. Don't you worry about what Michael might do. I'll take care of this. It's important for

you to remember that you should never let
anyone take your picture unless there's a good
reason for it."

Robyn knew that, and she knew that going
along with Michael for even one picture was a
mistake. But she knew that she did the right
thing after that, and she was glad she told her
mom what happened.

What would you do?

# WALT'S STORY

Walt was having a difficult time in third grade. He was doing all right in some subjects. Others were difficult for him.

He was trying very hard, and his mom and dad helped him when they could, but Walt was struggling.

One day in his arithmetic class, Mrs. Gardner, his teacher, wrote some numbers on the blackboard and asked Walt to multiply them and give the answer.

Walt thought one of the numbers was 28, but he wasn't sure. Maybe it was 23. He asked Mrs. Gardner what the number was. Mrs. Gardner told him it was 23. Then she said, "Walter, if you have trouble reading that number, I think you should tell your parents to have your eyes checked."

On the way home, Walt was upset. He didn't want to tell his parents what Mrs. Gardner said. He didn't want to wear glasses. What would his friends think? How could he play football?

Walt decided not to tell his parents. After all,

he thought, maybe Mrs. Gardner just didn't write
very clearly. But then he thought, "Maybe I do
need glasses. Could that be why I'm having
trouble in school?" With a heavy heart, he finally
decided to tell his dad what Mrs. Gardner said.

When his dad heard the whole story, he said, "Walt, we're going to have your eyes checked tomorrow. If you need glasses, it's important that you get them. As for playing football, do you have any idea how many pro players wear glasses or contact lenses?" His dad mentioned the names of three or four great football players.

Walt said, "Gee, they wear glasses? I didn't know that."

Walt felt better immediately. He was glad he told his dad about what Mrs. Gardner said. He decided that keeping it a secret might have been a dumb thing to do.

What would you do?

# NICOLE'S STORY

Nicole loved her ballet classes. She dreamed that when she grew up, she was going to be a great ballerina.

Mr. Johnston, her ballet teacher, was very encouraging. He told Nicole that she was very good for her age. One day, he asked Nicole if she would like to stay after class for special instruction.

Nicole was very pleased. She agreed to stay after class. Mr. Johnston taught her some new dance steps, but after a while, he started behaving very strangely. He began touching Nicole in ways she didn't like. She felt very uncomfortable. She thought she couldn't do anything to insult Mr. Johnston, because then he would stop giving her special attention.

But then she realized that Mr. Johnston was wrong to do what he was doing. She told him, "I don't want you to touch me anymore. I'm going home."

Nicole cried all the way home. She thought her dream of being a ballerina was over for good. At

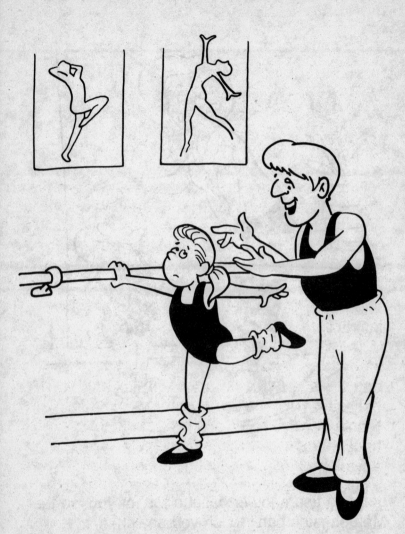

first, she didn't want to tell her mom about what happened. Finally, she realized that she should.

Her mom said, "Nicole, I'm glad you told me. No one has the right to touch you like that. I'm

going to find another ballet class for you, so that
Mr. Johnston can't touch you again."

Nicole was happy. She had her dream of
being a ballerina again. She was glad she told
her mom what happened.

What would you do?

# MATTHEW'S STORY

Matthew had a good friend, Billy. Billy was the only other boy Matthew knew who shared his interest in building model airplanes. They both especially liked building models of World War I planes. They were really good at getting all the details right.

One day, they were working in Billy's room when Billy started to cry. Matthew was stunned because it happened for no apparent reason. He asked his friend what was wrong. Billy pulled himself together and insisted that he was all right.

Matthew said, "Hey, I'm your friend. You can tell me anything. Maybe I can help."

Billy broke down and told Matthew what was bothering him. Billy's uncle was doing something to Billy that made him feel sick, but Billy said he was afraid of his uncle and scared to tell his parents.

Billy asked Matthew to swear to keep what he said a secret. Matthew said he would.

When Matthew got home that evening, Billy

was on his mind. He thought about how badly his friend was being hurt, and about his promise to keep Billy's conversation a secret.

The more Matthew thought about it, the more upset he felt about Billy. When he was on the verge of tears himself, Matthew went to his dad, told him Billy's story and how Billy had sworn him to secrecy.

Matthew's dad said, "Matthew, you've done the right thing. To keep Billy's secret would be to cause more and more pain for both of you. Billy has to have help. Deep down inside, he knows that. That's really why he told you. Tomorrow, I want you to tell Billy that you've spoken to me.

You may think it's going to end your friendship, but I don't think it will.

"Tomorrow, I'm going to talk with some people who can help, and we'll arrange to put Billy in contact with them. Matthew, you may never know how much this will help Billy. I'm proud that you had the guts to tell a secret that should never have been kept."

What would you do?

# CORAL'S STORY

Coral was nine years old. Her mom and dad divorced when she was six, and her mom got married again. Her stepfather was okay. He treated her nicely and she liked him—although not as much as her real dad.

One evening when Coral's mom was out of the house at a club meeting, her stepfather came home late from work. Coral could tell right away that he had had a few drinks on the way home. Coral hated it when adults smelled of alcohol.

Coral was sitting on the couch, watching television. Her stepfather sat down next to her and talked to her. Coral didn't like what he was saying. Then he leaned over, grabbed her by the shoulders, and kissed her hard on the mouth.

Coral was shocked. She pushed him away, got up quickly, ran to her room, and closed the door.

Coral was scared. She didn't know what to do. When her mom came home, she didn't say anything. She was afraid that if she told her

mom what happened, her mom would be mad at her. But she was also afraid that if she kept quiet, her stepfather would try to do the same thing again some other time.

After worrying about it all night, Coral told her mom the next morning, after her stepfather had left for work.

Her mom was upset, but she said to Coral, "Honey, this is not your fault. You didn't do anything that should make you feel guilty. My first responsibility is to protect you from anything like this. I'm going to talk to your stepfather about what happened, and I'll make sure it doesn't happen again."

Coral felt a lot better. She realized that it

wasn't her fault. She was glad she told her mom
what happened.

What would you do?

# ZACH'S STORY

Zach was seven years old and a Boy Scout. There was a group of older boys in his neighborhood, boys who hung around together and sometimes caused a lot of trouble.

One day, Zach had to walk past that group of boys on his way to a Boy Scout meeting. The biggest boy, Chris, who was about eleven, said, "Hey, Zach, from now on if you want to walk past us on this street, we're going to charge you a quarter. We're making this a 'toll street,' just like going over a bridge. Give us a quarter, or you're going to be stuck here all day."

Zach was scared. The boys were all a lot bigger than him. He gave Chris a quarter and went to the Scout meeting.

Zach didn't know what to do. He couldn't give the boys a quarter every time he walked down the street, but he thought they might hurt him if he didn't. And he couldn't take another street to his Boy Scout meetings, because that was the best way to get there. He thought about it and thought about it, and it really bothered him.

Finally, he told his mom about it. She said, "Zach, that is extortion, and that is a crime. Don't you worry about it. I'll put a stop to this very quickly."

Zach felt as though a big burden was lifted

from his shoulders and he was glad that he told
his mom what Chris and the other boys were
trying to do.

What would you do?

# LISA'S STORY

Most people don't like winter very much. Cold and snow can be uncomfortable. Lisa was different. She loved winter. She liked the cold. She was crazy about sledding and ice skating. In fact, Lisa sometimes thought that when she grew up, she'd move to the North Pole.

Lisa was ice skating one day with her friend Dawn. Dawn wasn't very good at ice skating, but she tried very hard. She'd fall down, and get up, and fall down, and get up again.

That day, when Dawn fell down for about the hundredth time, a man came over and helped her up. He started talking to the two girls. The three of them were the only people on the skating rink.

The man started saying some weird things, talking about love and sex. Lisa said, "You shouldn't talk to us like that. We're going home." And they left.

As they were walking home, Lisa said to
Dawn, "I think I'd better tell my mom about this."
Dawn said, "Oh, no, you can't do that. That's
Danielle's father. She's in my class. You could

get him in big trouble."

Lisa thought about that very hard. But she knew that the man shouldn't say things like that to children.

She told her mom what happened. Her mom said, "You're right to tell me. Sometimes it's a lot braver to speak up than to stay silent. I'm proud of you and I'll take care of this."

Lisa felt good about telling her mom what happened.

What would you do?